RECORDED VERSIONS GUITAR

AUTHENTIC TRANSCRIPTIONS
WITH NOTES AND TABLATURE

ONE-X

Music transcriptions by Pete Billmann

ISBN-13: 978-1-4234-2139-9
ISBN-10: 1-4234-2139-6

HAL•LEONARD®
CORPORATION

7777 W. BLUEMOUND RD. P.O. BOX 13819 MILWAUKEE, WI 53213

Visit Hal Leonard Online at
www.halleonard.com

In Australia Contact:
Hal Leonard Australia Pty. Ltd.
4 Lentara Court
Cheltenham, Victoria, 3192 Australia
Email: **ausadmin@halleonard.com**

It's All Over

Words and Music by Neil Sanderson, Adam Gontier, Brad Walst and Barry Stock

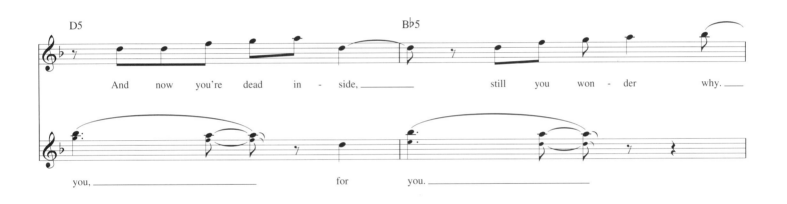

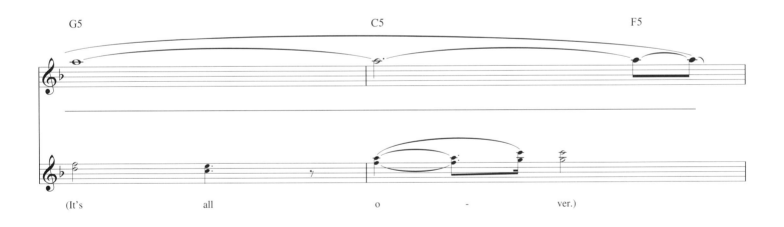

Pain

Words and Music by Neil Sanderson, Adam Gontier, Brad Walst, Gavin Brown and Barry Stock

Drop D tuning:
(low to high) D-A-D-G-B-E

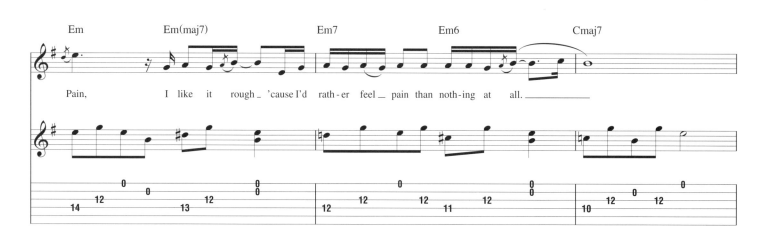

Verse

Gtrs. 2 & 3 tacet

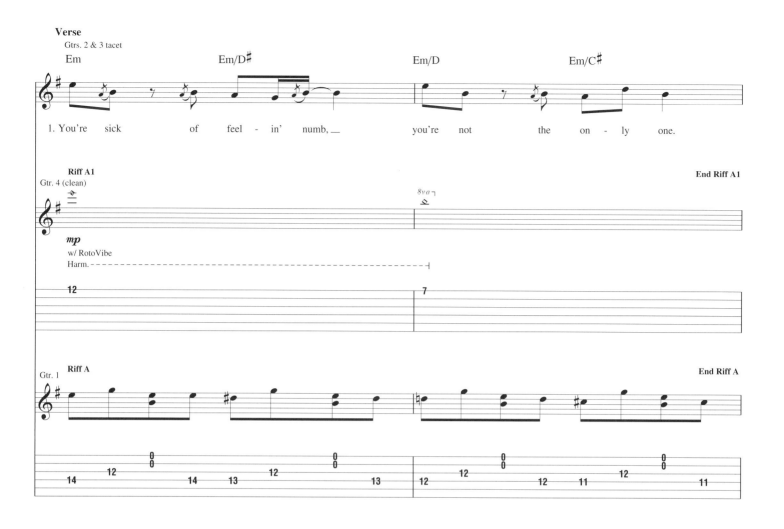

1. You're sick of feel-in' numb, ___ you're not the on-ly one.

Gtrs. 1 & 4: w/ Riffs A & A1 (3 times)

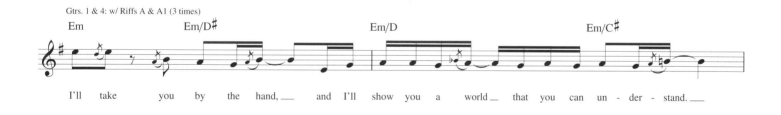

I'll take you by the hand, ___ and I'll show you a world ___ that you can un-der-stand. ___

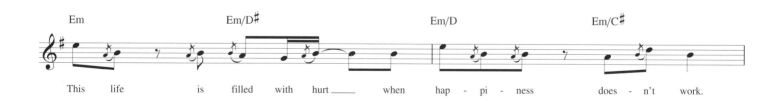

This life is filled with hurt ___ when hap-pi-ness does-n't work.

Trust me and take my hand. ___ When the lights go out you'll un-der-stand. ___

Trust me, I've got a plan. When the lights go up, you'll un-der-stand,

𝄋 Chorus

Gtr. 1: w/ Rhy. Fill 1
Gtr. 4: w/ Fill 1

Bkgd. Voc.: w/ Voc. Fig. 1 (2 times)
Gtrs. 1 & 4 tacet
Gtrs. 2 & 3: w/ Rhy. Figs. 1 & 1A (1 3/4 times)
2nd time, Gtr. 5 tacet

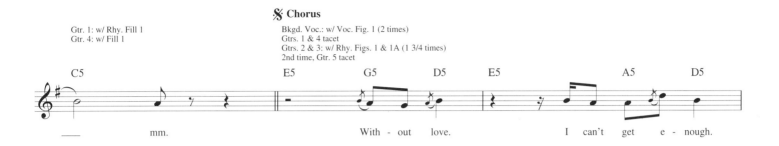

mm.   With - out love.   I can't get e - nough.

I like it rough __ 'cause I'd rath - er feel __ pain than noth - ing at all. __

To Coda ⊕

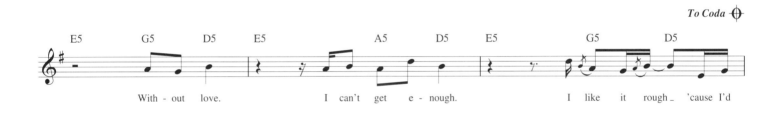

With - out love.   I can't get e - nough.   I like it rough __ 'cause I'd

rath - er feel __ pain than noth - ing, __ rath - er feel __ pain. __

Bridge

(I know, I know, I know,__ I know.

I know that you're wound - ed.

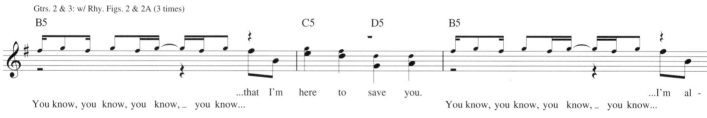

Gtrs. 2 & 3: w/ Rhy. Figs. 2 & 2A (3 times)

...that I'm here to save you.

You know, you know, you know,__ you know...

...I'm al -

You know, you know, you know,__ you know...

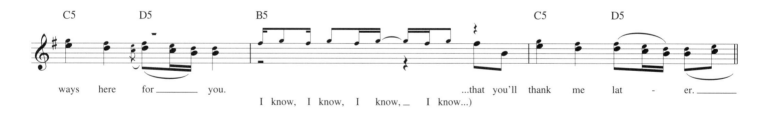

ways here for_____ you.

...that you'll thank me lat - er._____

I know, I know, I know,__ I know...)

Interlude

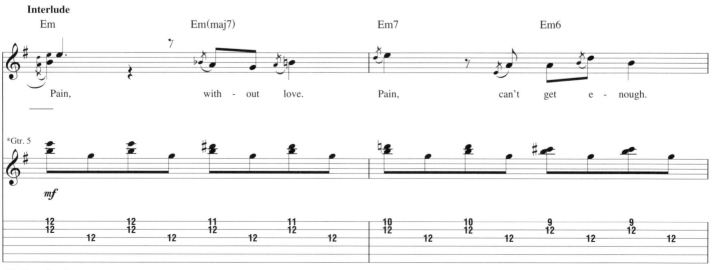

Pain, with - out love.

Pain, can't get e - nough.

*Gtr. 5

*Synth arr. for gtr.

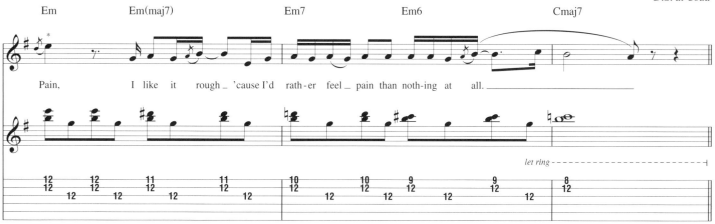

*Doubled w/ spoken vocal (next 3 meas.).

Coda

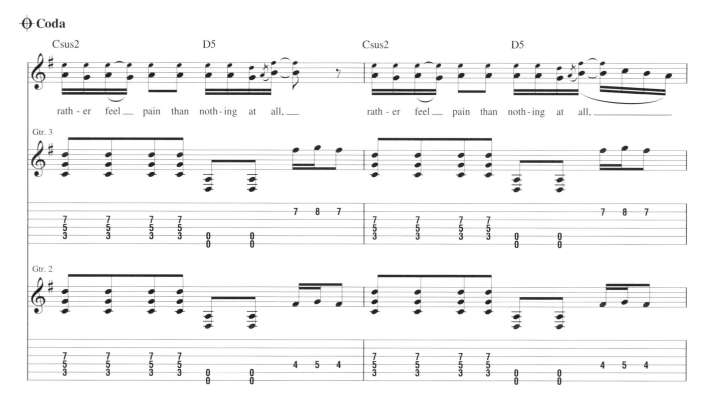

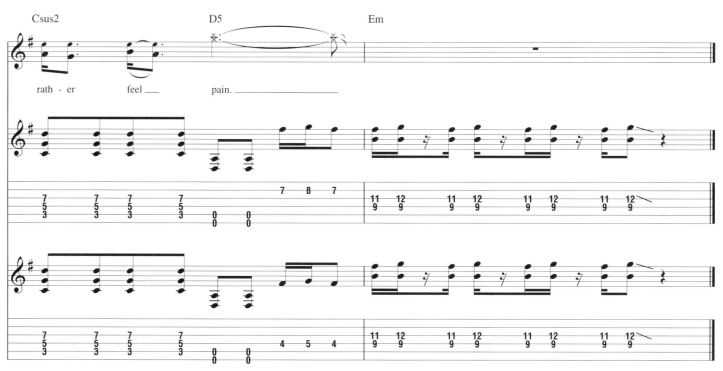

Animal I Have Become

Words and Music by Neil Sanderson, Adam Gontier, Brad Walst, Gavin Brown and Barry Stock

Some - bod - y wake me from this night - mare.
(Some - bod - y wake me from this night - mare.)

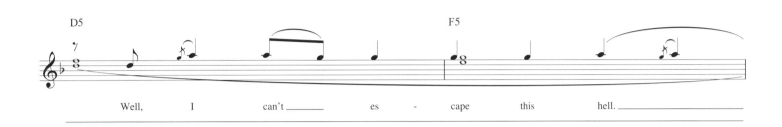

Well, I can't _____ es - cape this hell. _____

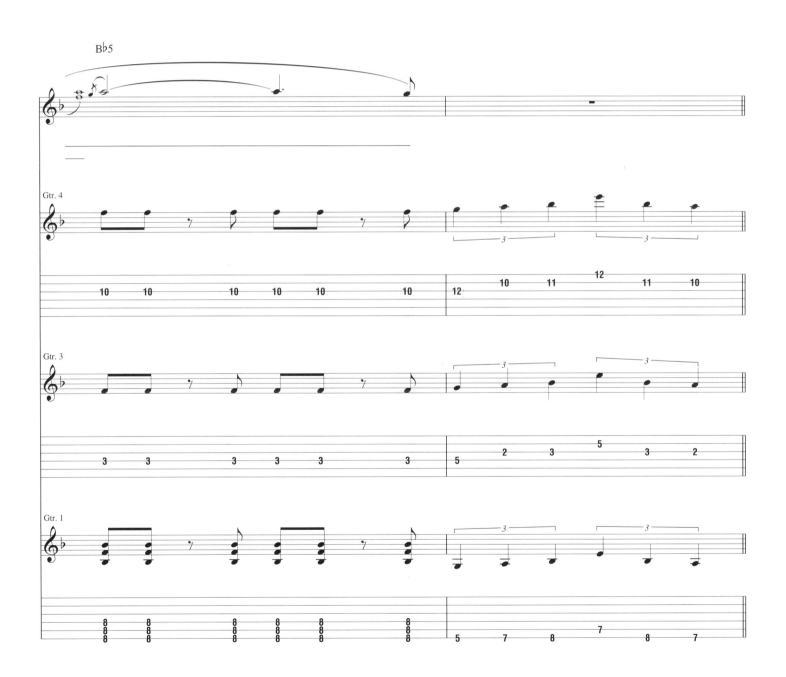

Interlude

D5

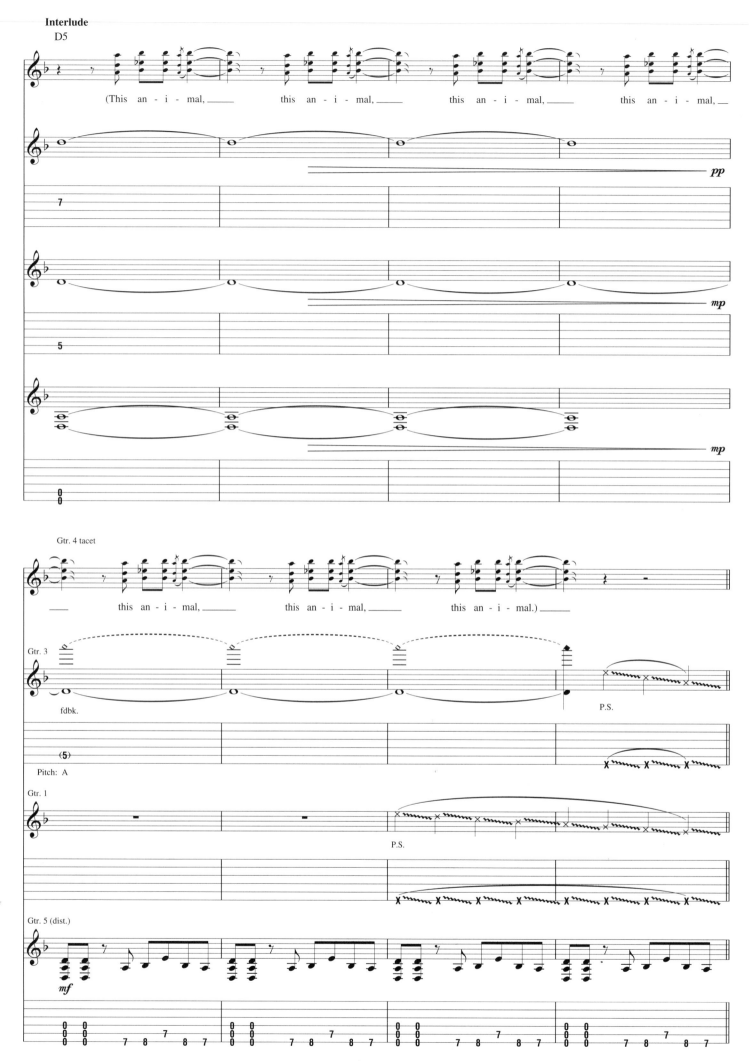

(This an - i - mal, ___ this an - i - mal, ___ this an - i - mal, ___ this an - i - mal, ___

Gtr. 4 tacet

this an - i - mal, ___ this an - i - mal, ___ this an - i - mal.) ___

Gtr. 3

fdbk.

P.S.

Pitch: A

Gtr. 1

P.S.

Gtr. 5 (dist.)

Never Too Late

Words and Music by Neil Sanderson, Adam Gontier, Brad Walst and Gavin Brown

And __ if there's some - thing wrong, __ who would-'ve guessed __ it? __

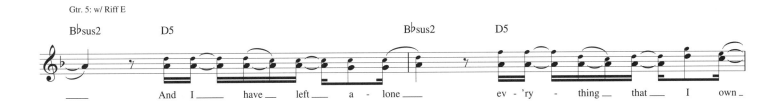

And I __ have __ left __ a - lone __ ev - 'ry - thing __ that __ I own __

to make __ you feel __ like it's not too late. It's nev - er too late. __

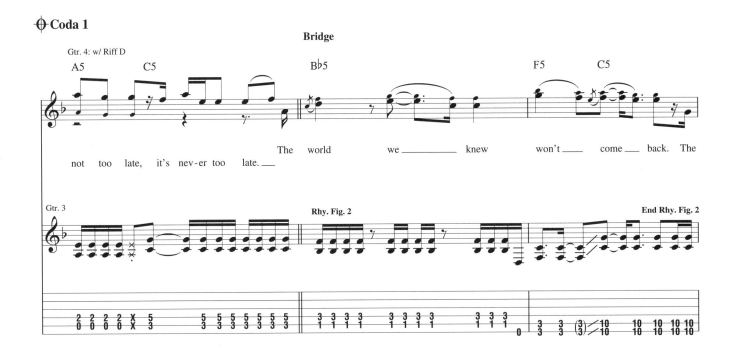

not too late, it's nev-er too late. __   The world we __ knew won't __ come __ back. The

On My Own

Words and Music by Neil Sanderson, Adam Gontier, Brad Walst, Gavin Brown and Barry Stock

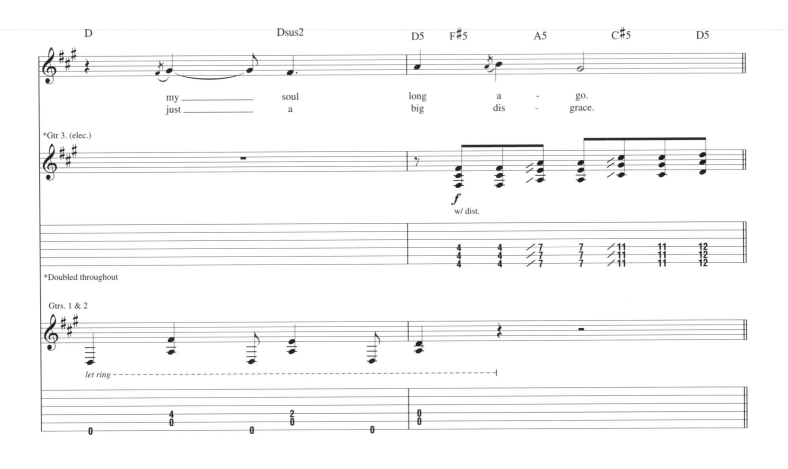

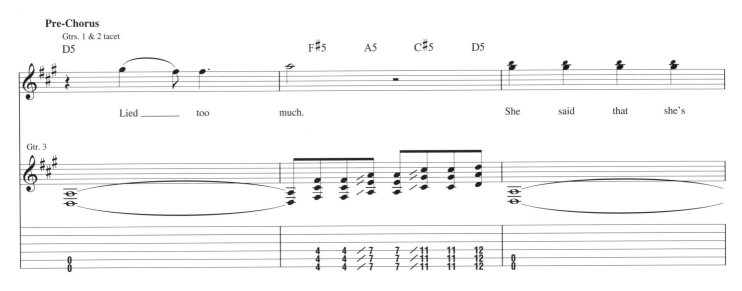

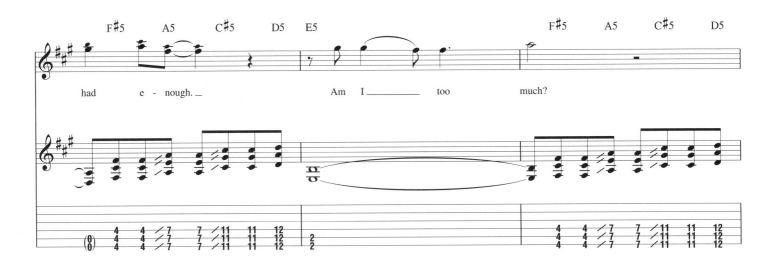

Riot

Words and Music by Neil Sanderson, Adam Gontier, Brad Walst and Barry Stock

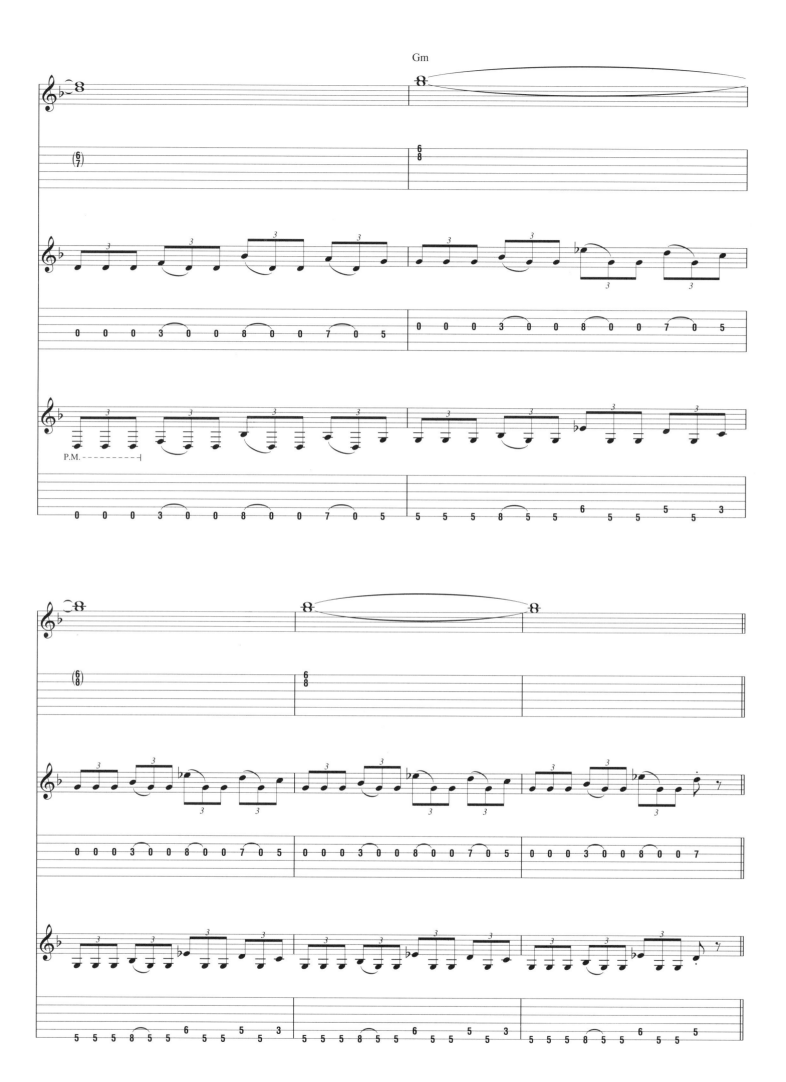

Verse
Half-time feel

Gtrs. 3, 4 & 5 tacet

3. If you ___ feel so emp - ty, so used ___ up, so let ___ down,

if you ___ feel so an - gry, just get ___ up. ___

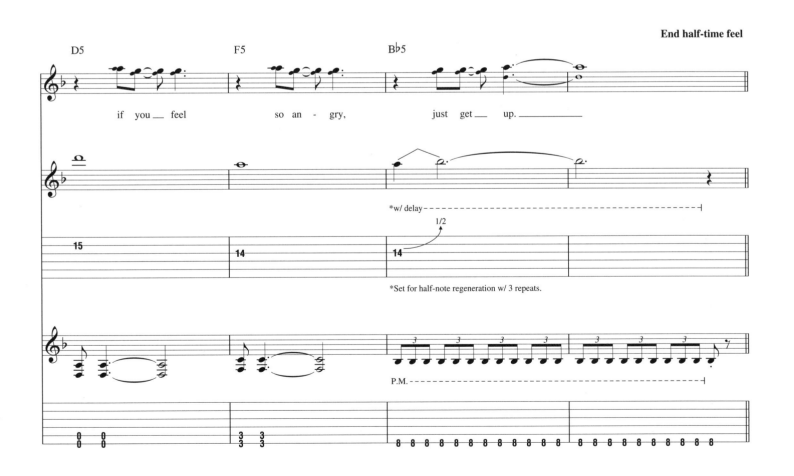

Get Out Alive

Words and Music by Neil Sanderson, Adam Gontier, Brad Walst and Barry Stock

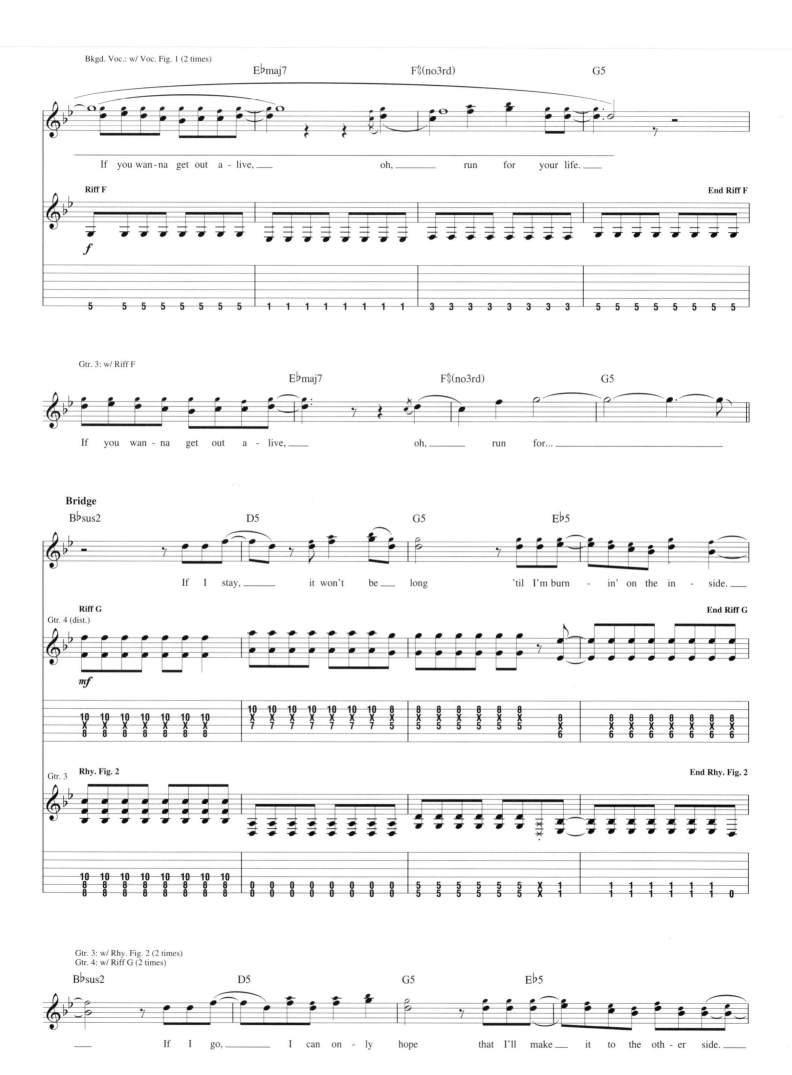

If I stay, _____ it won't be _____ long 'til I'm burn - in' on the in - side. _____

If I go, _____ and if I ____ go...

Gtr. 4

mf

Gtr. 3

Outro

Gtr. 3: w/ Rhy. Fig. 1 (3 times)

Burn - in' on the in - side. _____

Riff H

Gtr. 4

End Riff H

Gtr. 4: w/ Riff H

Burn - in' on the in - side. _____

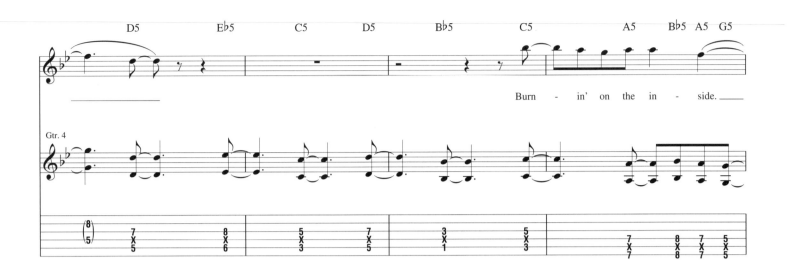

Burn - in' on the in - side. ____

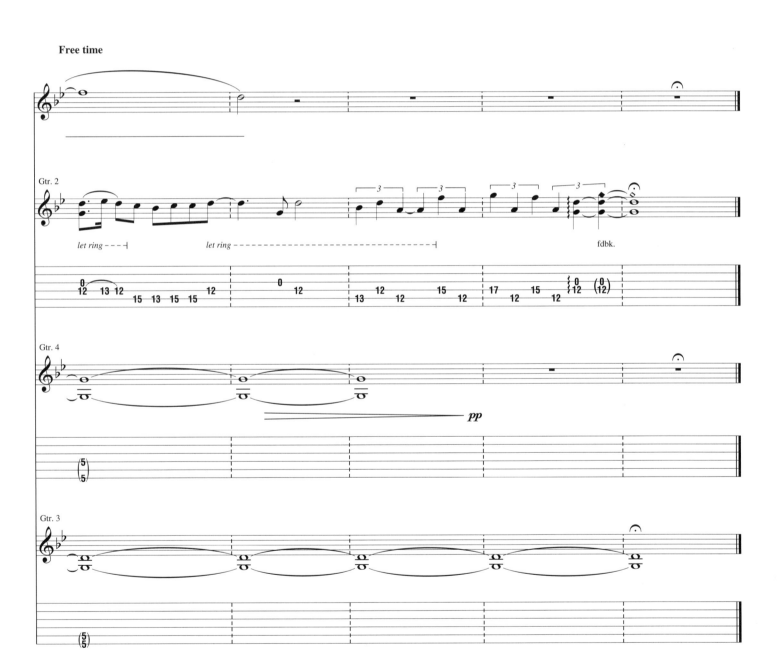

Free time

Let It Die

Words and Music by Neil Sanderson, Adam Gontier, Brad Walst, Gavin Brown and Barry Stock

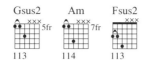

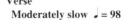

Drop D tuning:
(low to high) D-A-D-G-B-E

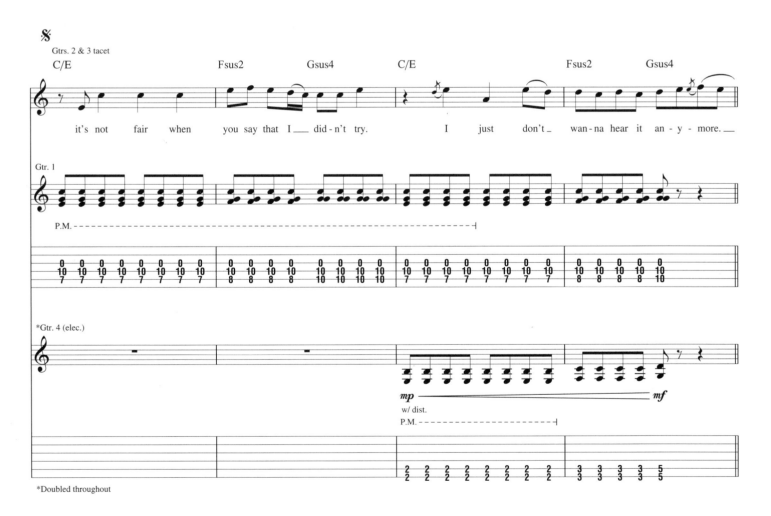

*Doubled throughout

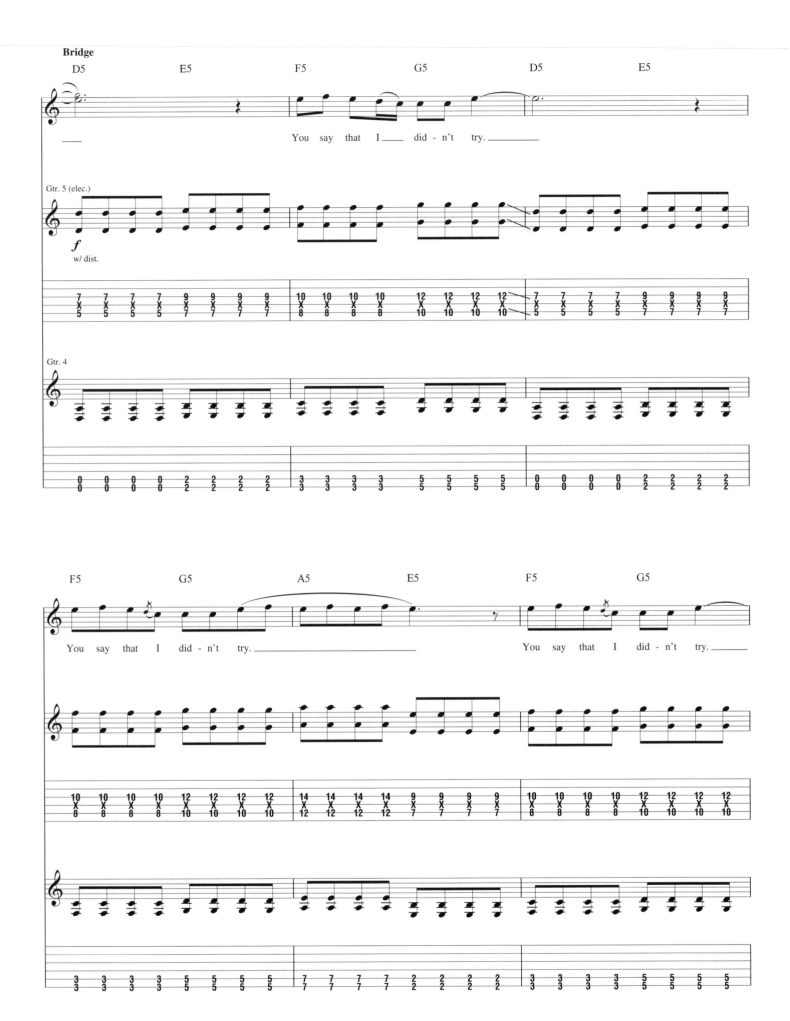

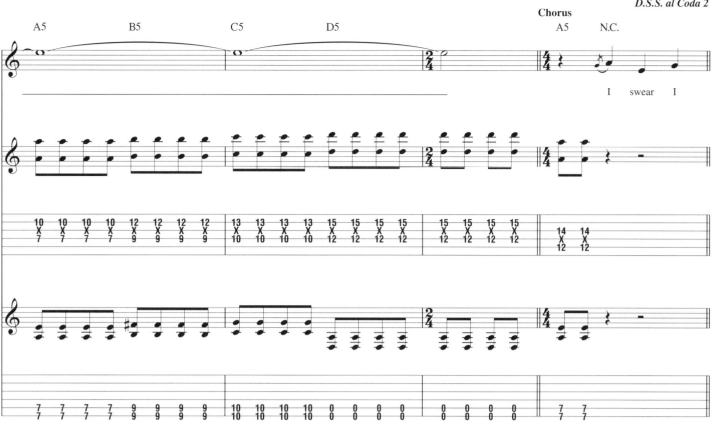

Chorus

A5   B5   C5   D5   A5   N.C.

I swear I

Coda 2

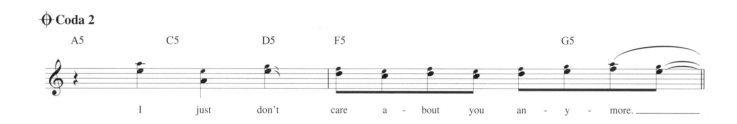

A5   C5   D5   F5   G5

I just don't care a-bout you an - y - more.

Outro-Chorus

Gtr. 4: w/ Rhy. Fig. 4 (1 1/2 times)

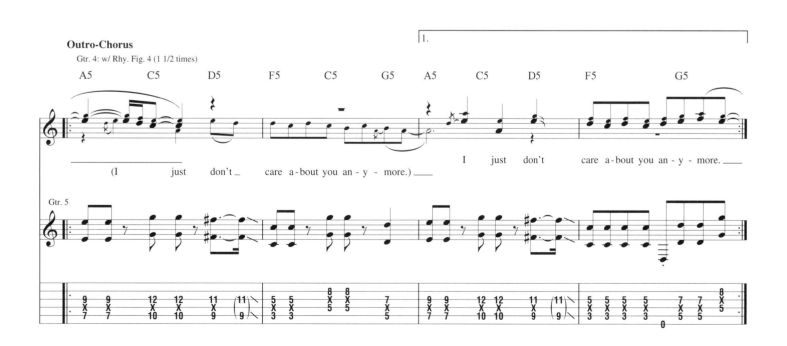

A5   C5   D5   F5   C5   G5   A5   C5   D5   F5   G5

(I just don't__ care a-bout you an - y - more.)__ I just don't care a-bout you an - y - more.__

Gtr. 5

I just don't care a - bout you an - y - more.

Free time

Over and Over

Words and Music by Neil Sanderson, Adam Gontier, Brad Walst, Gavin Brown and Barry Stock

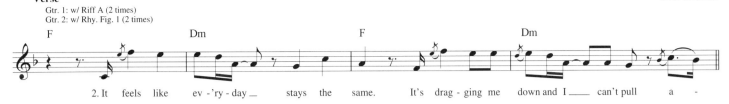

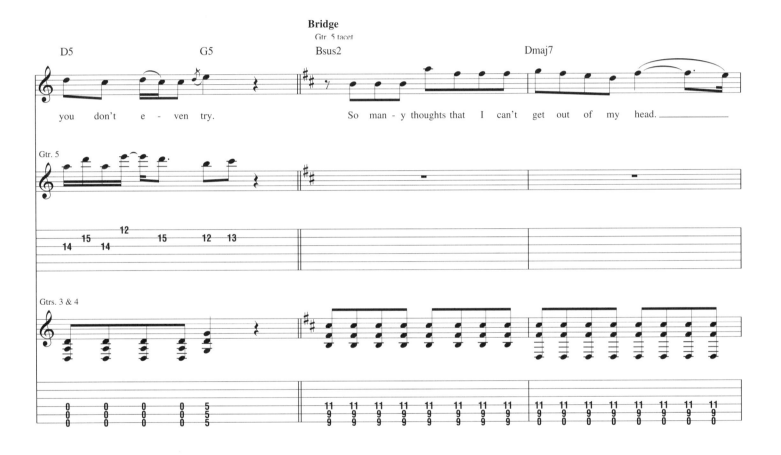

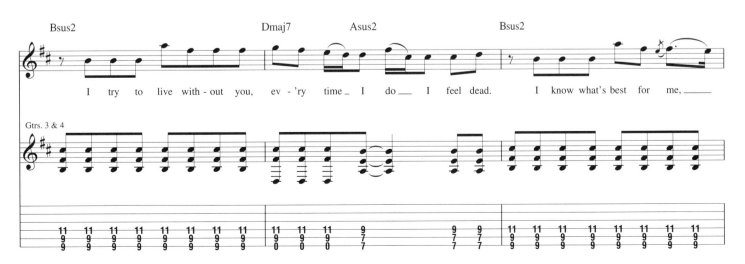

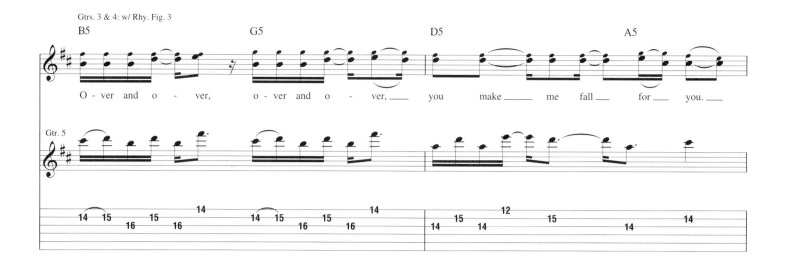

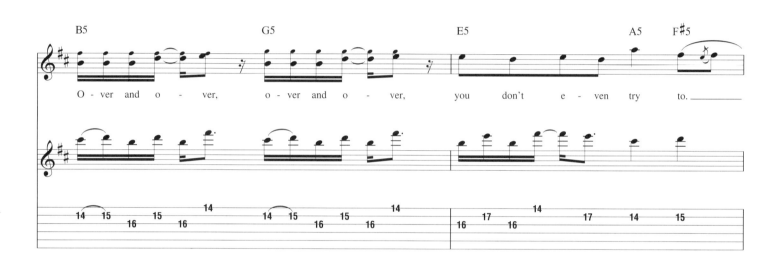

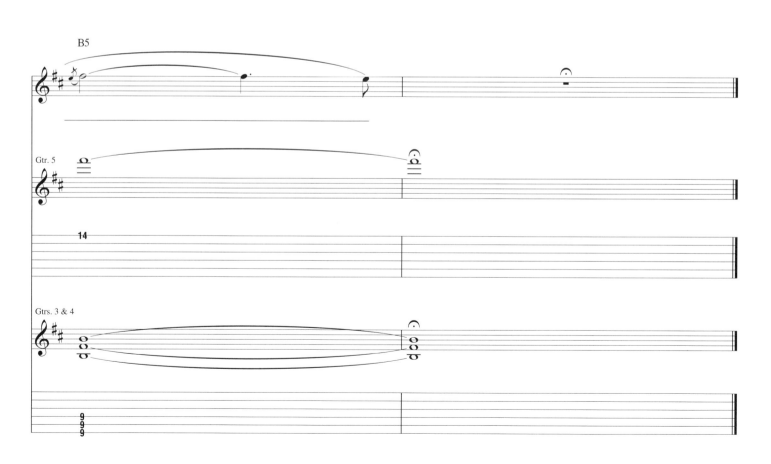

Time of Dying

Words and Music by Neil Sanderson, Adam Gontier, Brad Walst and Barry Stock

Drop D tuning, down 1 step:
(low to high) C-G-C-F-A-D

Intro
Moderately ♩ = 100

*Gtr. 1 (dist.)

*Doubled throughout
Gtr. 2 (dist.)

**Chord symbols reflect implied harmony.

Pitch: C
***Microphonic fdbk.,
not caused by
string vibration.

Rhy. Fig. 1
Gtrs. 1 & 2
loco

End Rhy. Fig. 1

Verse
Gtr. 2 tacet

1. On — the ground I — lay mo-tion-less, in — pain. I — can see my — life flash-ing — be-fore my — eyes.

Gtr. 3 (slight dist.)

f
w/ RotoVibe

Gtr. 1

Gone Forever

Words and Music by Neil Sanderson, Adam Gontier, Brad Walst, Gavin Brown and Barry Stock

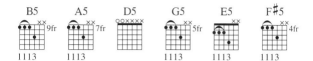

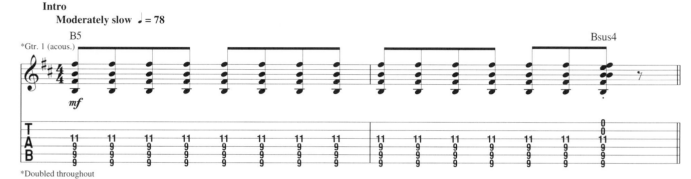

Gtrs. 1-9: Drop D tuning:
(low to high) D-A-D-G-B-E

Gtr. 10 tuning:
(low to high) D-A-D-F♯-B-D

Intro
Moderately slow ♩ = 78

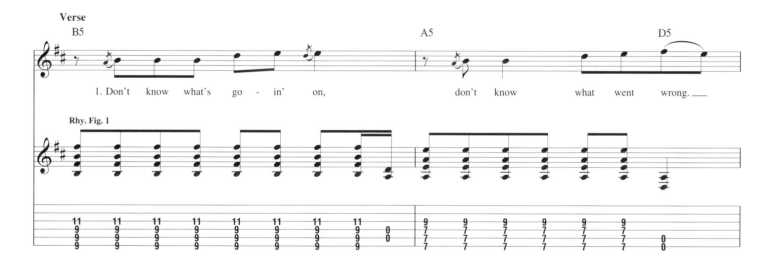

Verse

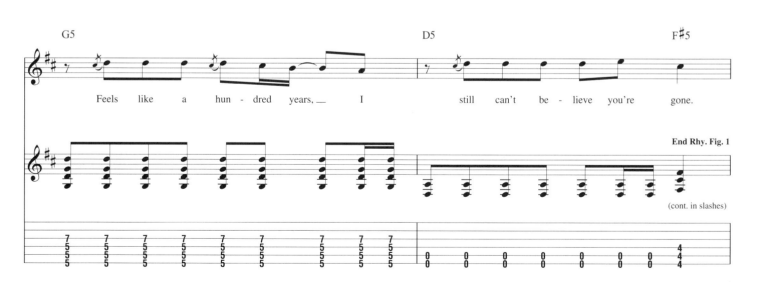

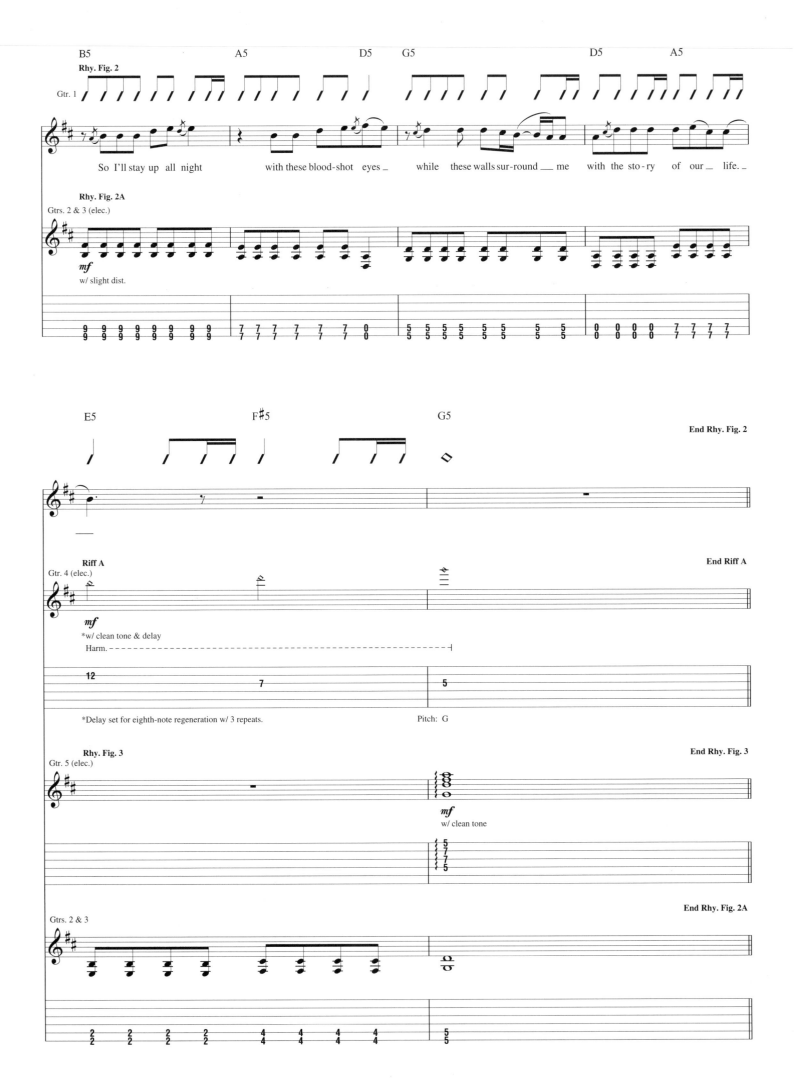

So I'll stay up all night   with these blood-shot eyes _   while these walls sur-round _ me   with the sto - ry   of our _   life. _

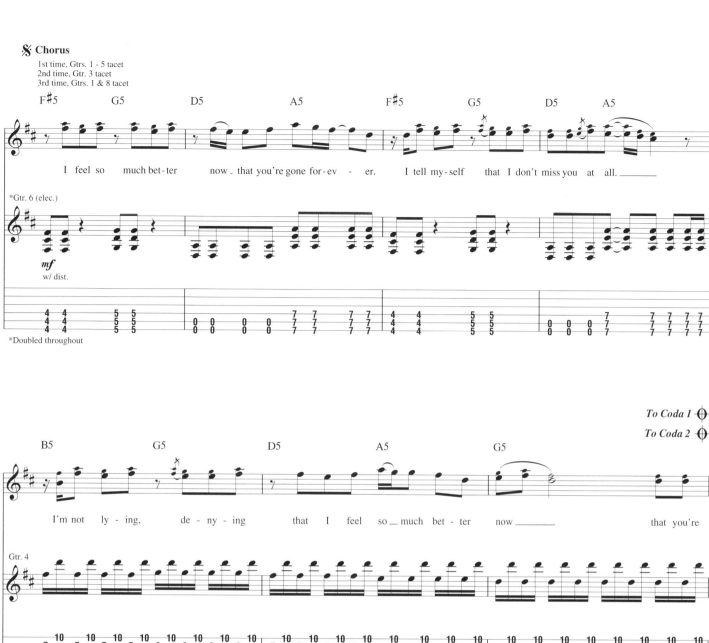

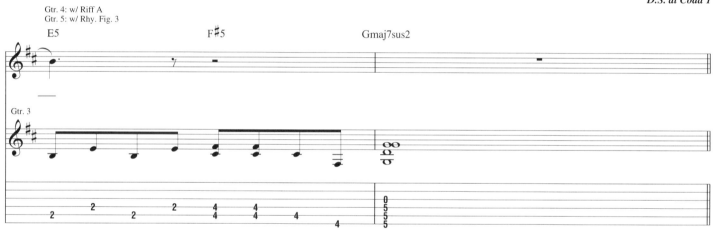

D.S. al Coda 1

Coda 1

Bridge

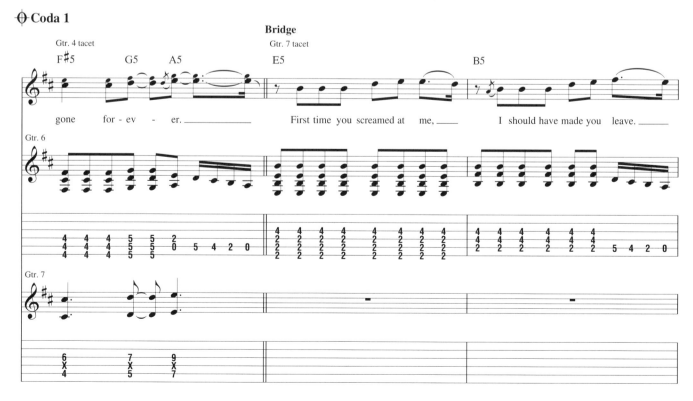

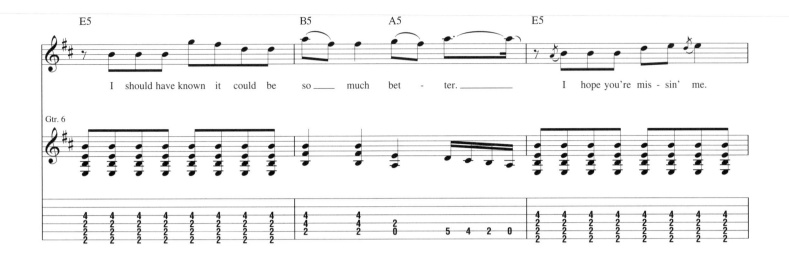

I should have known it could be so ___ much bet - ter. ___ I hope you're mis - sin' me.

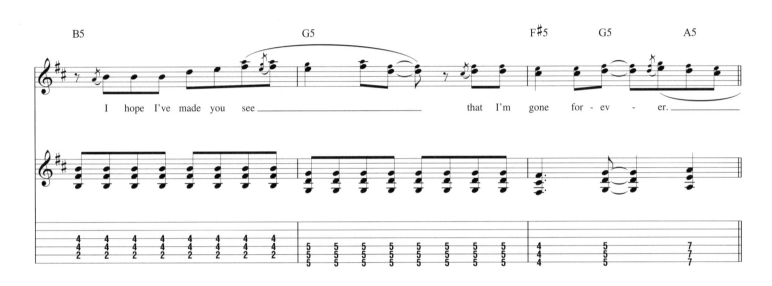

I hope I've made you see ___ that I'm gone for - ev - er. ___

Verse

Gtr. 1: w/ Rhy. Fig. 1 (1st 2 meas.)

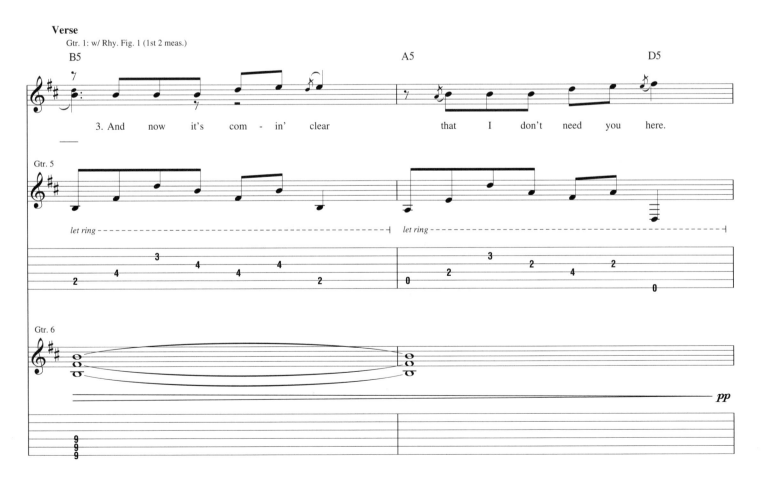

3. And now it's com - in' clear that I don't need you here.

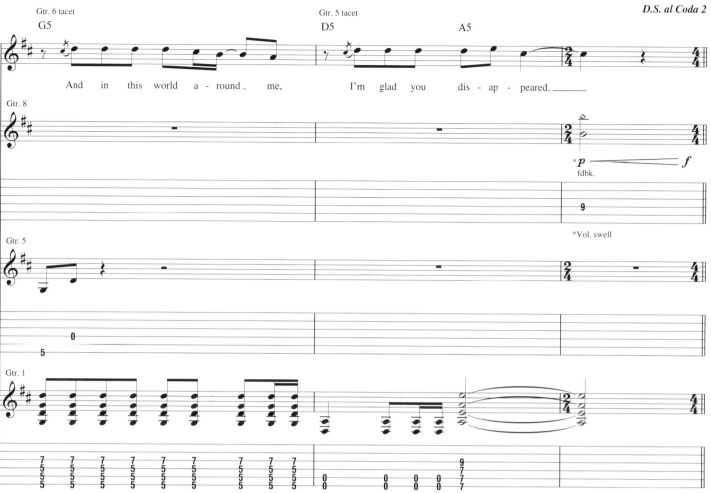

Coda 2

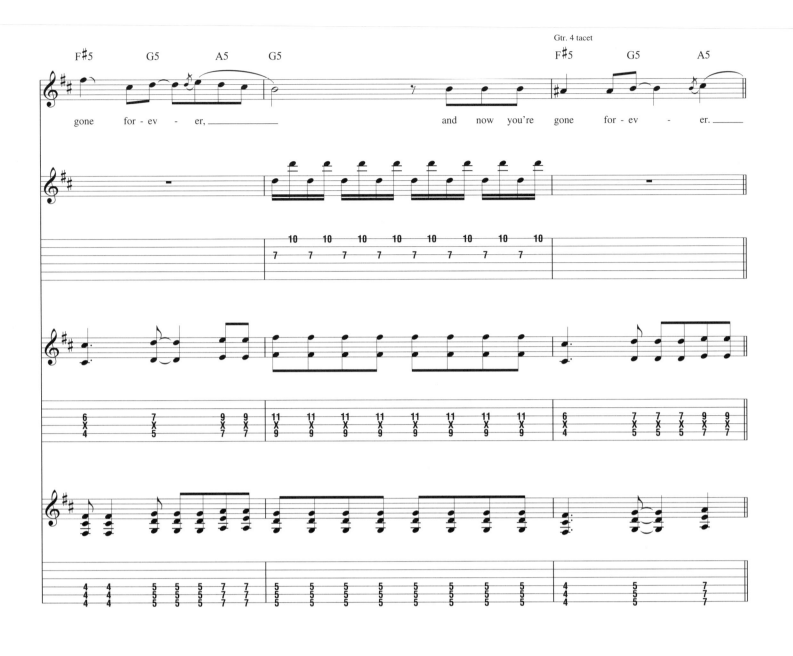

Outro

One-X

Words and Music by Neil Sanderson, Adam Gontier, Brad Walst and Barry Stock

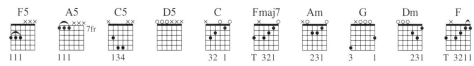

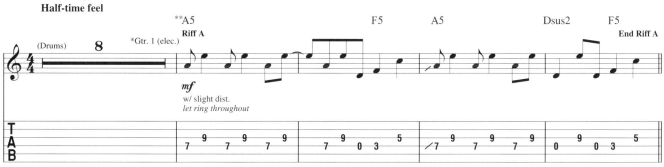

Drop D tuning:
(low to high) D-A-D-G-B-E

Intro
Moderately ♩ = 128
Half-time feel

*Doubled throughout

**Chord symbols reflect implied harmony.

1. Do you think a-bout ev-'ry-thing you've been through? You nev-er thought you'd be so de-pressed.

Are you won-der-ing is it life or death? Do you think that there's no one like you?

Pre-Chorus

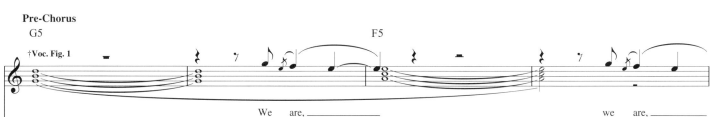

We are, we are,

(Oo,

***Gtr. 2 (elec.) w/ clean tone & RotoVibe, played *mf*.

†Refers to bkgd. voc. only.

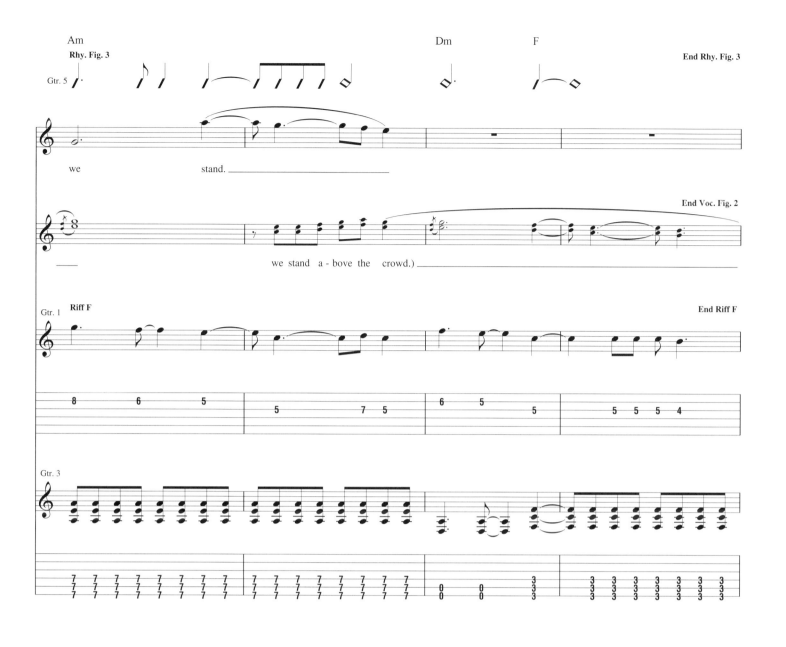

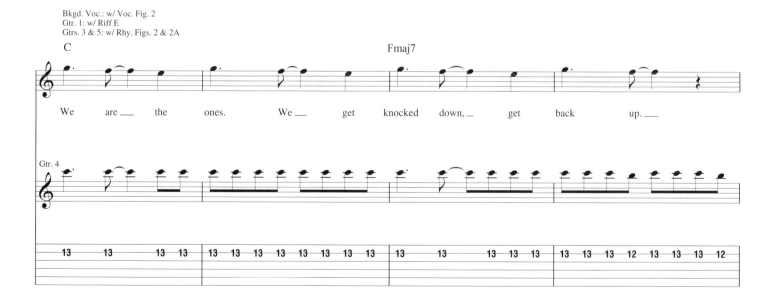

Guitar Notation Legend

Guitar music can be notated three different ways: on a *musical staff*, in *tablature*, and in *rhythm slashes*.

RHYTHM SLASHES are written above the staff. Strum chords in the rhythm indicated. Use the chord diagrams found at the top of the first page of the transcription for the appropriate chord voicings. Round noteheads indicate single notes.

THE MUSICAL STAFF shows pitches and rhythms and is divided by bar lines into measures. Pitches are named after the first seven letters of the alphabet.

TABLATURE graphically represents the guitar fingerboard. Each horizontal line represents a string, and each number represents a fret.

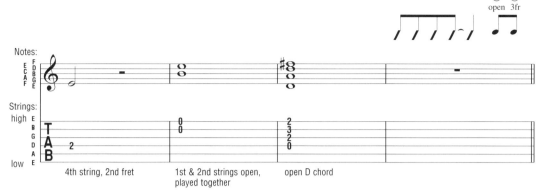

4th string, 2nd fret

1st & 2nd strings open, played together

open D chord

HALF-STEP BEND: Strike the note and bend up 1/2 step.

WHOLE-STEP BEND: Strike the note and bend up one step.

GRACE NOTE BEND: Strike the note and immediately bend up as indicated.

SLIGHT (MICROTONE) BEND: Strike the note and bend up 1/4 step.

BEND AND RELEASE: Strike the note and bend up as indicated, then release back to the original note. Only the first note is struck.

PRE-BEND: Bend the note as indicated, then strike it.

VIBRATO: The string is vibrated by rapidly bending and releasing the note with the fretting hand.

WIDE VIBRATO: The pitch is varied to a greater degree by vibrating with the fretting hand.

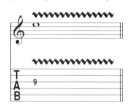

HAMMER-ON: Strike the first (lower) note with one finger, then sound the higher note (on the same string) with another finger by fretting it without picking.

PULL-OFF: Place both fingers on the notes to be sounded. Strike the first note and without picking, pull the finger off to sound the second (lower) note.

LEGATO SLIDE: Strike the first note and then slide the same fret-hand finger up or down to the second note. The second note is not struck.

SHIFT SLIDE: Same as legato slide, except the second note is struck.

TRILL: Very rapidly alternate between the notes indicated by continuously hammering on and pulling off.

TAPPING: Hammer ("tap") the fret indicated with the pick-hand index or middle finger and pull off to the note fretted by the fret hand.

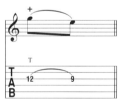

NATURAL HARMONIC: Strike the note while the fret-hand lightly touches the string directly over the fret indicated.

PINCH HARMONIC: The note is fretted normally and a harmonic is produced by adding the edge of the thumb or the tip of the index finger of the pick hand to the normal pick attack.

PICK SCRAPE: The edge of the pick is rubbed down (or up) the string, producing a scratchy sound.

MUFFLED STRINGS: A percussive sound is produced by laying the fret hand across the string(s) without depressing, and striking them with the pick hand.

PALM MUTING: The note is partially muted by the pick hand lightly touching the string(s) just before the bridge.

RAKE: Drag the pick across the strings indicated with a single motion.

TREMOLO PICKING: The note is picked as rapidly and continuously as possible.

VIBRATO BAR DIVE AND RETURN: The pitch of the note or chord is dropped a specified number of steps (in rhythm), then returned to the original pitch.

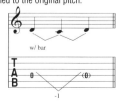

VIBRATO BAR SCOOP: Depress the bar just before striking the note, then quickly release the bar.

VIBRATO BAR DIP: Strike the note and then immediately drop a specified number of steps, then release back to the original pitch.

RECORDED VERSIONS®
The Best Note-For-Note Transcriptions Available

ALL BOOKS INCLUDE TABLATURE

00692015 Aerosmith – Greatest Hits $22.95	00690602 Hendrix, Jimi – Smash Hits $19.95	00690379 Red Hot Chili Peppers – Californication . .$19.95
00690603 Aerosmith – O Yeah! (Ultimate Hits) $24.95	00690692 Idol, Billy – Very Best of $19.95	00690673 Red Hot Chili Peppers – Greatest Hits $19.95
00690178 Alice in Chains – Acoustic $19.95	00690688 Incubus – A Crow Left of the Murder $19.95	00690511 Reinhardt, Django – Definitive Collection . .$19.95
00694865 Alice in Chains – Dirt $19.95	00690457 Incubus – Make Yourself $19.95	00690779 Relient K – MMHMM $19.95
00690387 Alice in Chains – Nothing Safe:	00690544 Incubus – Morningview $19.95	00690643 Relient K – Two Lefts Don't
The Best of the Box $19.95	00690730 Jackson, Alan – Guitar Collection $19.95	Make a Right...But Three Do $19.95
00690812 All American Rejects – Move Along $19.95	00690721 Jet – Get Born $19.95	00690631 Rolling Stones – Guitar Anthology $24.95
00694932 Allman Brothers Band – Volume 1 . . . . .$24.95	00690684 Jethro Tull – Aqualung $19.95	00690685 Roth, David Lee – Eat 'Em and Smile $19.95
00694933 Allman Brothers Band – Volume 2 . . . . .$24.95	00690647 Jewel – Best of $19.95	00690694 Roth, David Lee – Guitar Anthology $24.95
00694934 Allman Brothers Band – Volume 3 . . . . .$24.95	00690751 John5 – Vertigo $19.95	00690749 Saliva – Survival of the Sickest $19.95
00690755 Alter Bridge – One Day Remains $19.95	00690271 Johnson, Robert – New Transcriptions . .$24.95	00690031 Santana's Greatest Hits $19.95
00690609 Audioslave $19.95	00699131 Joplin, Janis – Best of $19.95	00690796 Schenker, Michael – Very Best of $19.95
00690804 Audioslave – Out of Exile $19.95	00690427 Judas Priest – Best of $19.95	00690566 Scorpions – Best of $19.95
00690366 Bad Company – Original Anthology, Book 1 . .$19.95	00690742 Killers, The – Hot Fuss $19.95	00690604 Seger, Bob – Guitar Collection $19.95
00690503 Beach Boys – Very Best of $19.95	00694903 Kiss – Best of $24.95	00690530 Slipknot – Iowa $19.95
00690489 Beatles – 1 . . . .$24.95	00690780 Korn – Greatest Hits, Volume 1 . . . .$22.95	00690733 Slipknot – Vol. 3 (The Subliminal Verses) . .$19.95
00694929 Beatles – 1962-1966 . . . .$24.95	00690726 Lavigne, Avril – Under My Skin $19.95	00690691 Smashing Pumpkins Anthology $19.95
00694930 Beatles – 1967-1970 . . . .$24.95	00690679 Lennon, John – Guitar Collection $19.95	00120004 Steely Dan – Best of $24.95
00694832 Beatles – For Acoustic Guitar $22.95	00690785 Limp Bizkit – Best of $19.95	00694921 Steppenwolf – Best of $22.95
00690110 Beatles – White Album (Book 1) $19.95	00690781 Linkin Park – Hybrid Theory $22.95	00690655 Stern, Mike – Best of $19.95
00690792 Beck – Guero $19.95	00690782 Linkin Park – Meteora $22.95	00690689 Story of the Year – Page Avenue $19.95
00692385 Berry, Chuck $19.95	00690783 Live, Best of $19.95	00690520 Styx Guitar Collection $19.95
00692200 Black Sabbath –	00690743 Los Lonely Boys $19.95	00120081 Sublime $19.95
We Sold Our Soul for Rock 'N' Roll . .$19.95	00690720 Lostprophets – Start Something $19.95	00690519 SUM 41 – All Killer No Filler $19.95
00690674 Blink-182 . . . .$19.95	00694954 Lynyrd Skynyrd – New Best of $19.95	00690771 SUM 41 – Chuck $19.95
00690389 Blink-182 – Enema of the State $19.95	00690577 Malmsteen, Yngwie – Anthology $24.95	00690767 Switchfoot – The Beautiful Letdown $19.95
00690523 Blink-182 – Take Off Your Pants & Jacket . .$19.95	00690754 Manson, Marilyn – Lest We Forget $19.95	00690815 Switchfoot – Nothing Is Sound $19.95
00690491 Bowie, David – Best of $19.95	00694956 Marley, Bob – Legend $19.95	00690799 System of a Down – Mezmerize $19.95
00690764 Breaking Benjamin – We Are Not Alone . .$19.95	00694945 Marley, Bob – Songs of Freedom $24.95	00690531 System of a Down – Toxicity $19.95
00694951 Buckley, Jeff – Collection $24.95	00690748 Maroon5 – 1.22.03 Acoustic $19.95	00694824 Taylor, James – Best of $16.95
00690590 Clapton, Eric – Anthology $29.95	00690657 Maroon5 – Songs About Jane $19.95	00690737 3 Doors Down – The Better Life $22.95
00690415 Clapton Chronicles – Best of Eric Clapton . .$18.95	00120080 McLean, Don – Songbook $19.95	00690776 3 Doors Down – Seventeen Days $19.95
00690074 Clapton, Eric – The Cream of Clapton . . .$24.95	00694951 Megadeth – Rust in Peace $22.95	00690683 Trower, Robin – Bridge of Sighs $19.95
00690716 Clapton, Eric – Me and Mr. Johnson $19.95	00690768 Megadeth – The System Has Failed $19.95	00690740 Twain, Shania – Guitar Collection $19.95
00694869 Clapton, Eric – Unplugged $22.95	00690505 Mellencamp, John – Guitar Collection . . .$19.95	00699191 U2 – Best of: 1980-1990 . . . .$19.95
00690162 Clash – Best of The $19.95	00690646 Metheny, Pat – One Quiet Night $19.95	00690732 U2 – Best of: 1990-2000 . . . .$19.95
00690593 Coldplay – A Rush of Blood to the Head . .$19.95	00690565 Metheny, Pat – Rejoicing $19.95	00690775 U2 – How to Dismantle an Atomic Bomb . .$22.95
00690806 Coldplay – X & Y $19.95	00690558 Metheny, Pat – Trio: 99>00 . . . .$19.95	00694411 U2 – The Joshua Tree $19.95
00694940 Counting Crows – August & Everything After . .$19.95	00690561 Metheny, Pat – Trio > Live $22.95	00660137 Vai, Steve – Passion & Warfare $24.95
00690401 Creed – Human Clay $19.95	00690040 Miller, Steve, Band – Young Hearts $19.95	00690370 Vaughan, Stevie Ray and Double Trouble –
00690352 Creed – My Own Prison $19.95	00690769 Modest Mouse – Good News	The Real Deal: Greatest Hits Volume 2 . .$22.95
00690551 Creed – Weathered $19.95	for People Who Love Bad News . .$19.95	00690116 Vaughan, Stevie Ray – Guitar Collection . . .$24.95
00690648 Croce, Jim – Very Best of $19.95	00690786 Mudvayne – The End of All Things to Come . .$22.95	00660058 Vaughan, Stevie Ray –
00690572 Cropper, Steve – Soul Man $19.95	00690787 Mudvayne – L.D. 50 . . . .$22.95	Lightnin' Blues 1983-1987 . . . .$24.95
00690613 Crosby, Stills & Nash – Best of $19.95	00690794 Mudvayne – Lost and Found $19.95	00694835 Vaughan, Stevie Ray – The Sky Is Crying . .$22.95
00690777 Crossfade $19.95	00690611 Nirvana $22.95	00690015 Vaughan, Stevie Ray – Texas Flood $19.95
00690289 Deep Purple – Best of $17.95	00694883 Nirvana – Nevermind $19.95	00690772 Velvet Revolver – Contraband $22.95
00690347 Doors, The – Anthology $22.95	00690026 Nirvana – Unplugged in New York $19.95	00690071 Weezer (The Blue Album) $19.95
00690348 Doors, The – Essential Guitar Collection . .$16.95	00690739 No Doubt – Rock Steady $22.95	00690800 Weezer – Make Believe $19.95
00690810 Fall Out Boy – From Under the Cork Tree . .$19.95	00690807 Offspring, The – Greatest Hits $19.95	00690447 Who, The – Best of $24.95
00690664 Fleetwood Mac – Best of $19.95	00694847 Osbourne, Ozzy – Best of $22.95	00690672 Williams, Dar – Best of $19.95
00690808 Foo Fighters – In Your Honor $19.95	00690399 Osbourne, Ozzy – Ozzman Cometh $19.95	00690710 Yellowcard – Ocean Avenue $19.95
00694920 Free – Best of $19.95	00694855 Pearl Jam – Ten $19.95	00690589 ZZ Top Guitar Anthology $22.95
00690773 Good Charlotte –	00690439 Perfect Circle, A – Mer De Noms $19.95	
The Chronicles of Life and Death $19.95	00690661 Perfect Circle, A – Thirteenth Step $19.95	
00690601 Good Charlotte –	00690499 Petty, Tom – Definitive Guitar Collection . .$19.95	
The Young and the Hopeless $19.95	00690731 Pillar – Where Do We Go from Here? $19.95	
00690697 Hall, Jim – Best of $19.95	00690428 Pink Floyd – Dark Side of the Moon $19.95	
00694798 Harrison, George – Anthology $19.95	00693864 Police, The – Best of $19.95	
00690778 Hawk Nelson – Letters to the President . .$19.95	00694975 Queen – Greatest Hits $24.95	
00692930 Hendrix, Jimi – Are You Experienced? $24.95	00690670 Queensryche – Very Best of $19.95	
00692931 Hendrix, Jimi – Axis: Bold As Love $22.95	00694910 Rage Against the Machine $19.95	
00690608 Hendrix, Jimi – Blue Wild Angel $24.95	00690055 Red Hot Chili Peppers –	
00692932 Hendrix, Jimi – Electric Ladyland $24.95	Bloodsugarsexmagik $19.95	
00690017 Hendrix, Jimi – Live at Woodstock $24.95	00690584 Red Hot Chili Peppers – By the Way $19.95